UNFOLLOWING YOU

UNFOLLOWING YOU

KOMAL KAPOOR

For all the badasses reluctant to show their soft side—you are not alone.

There is this myth that showing emotions is a sign of weakness, a myth I believed for many years. This book is my way back to my feelings. To be comfortable with them, around them, in them. May it help you embrace yours as well.

And to anyone who struggles to talk about love and heartbreak, I hope you find the power in your vulnerability. It is okay to feel something; there is even strength in it.

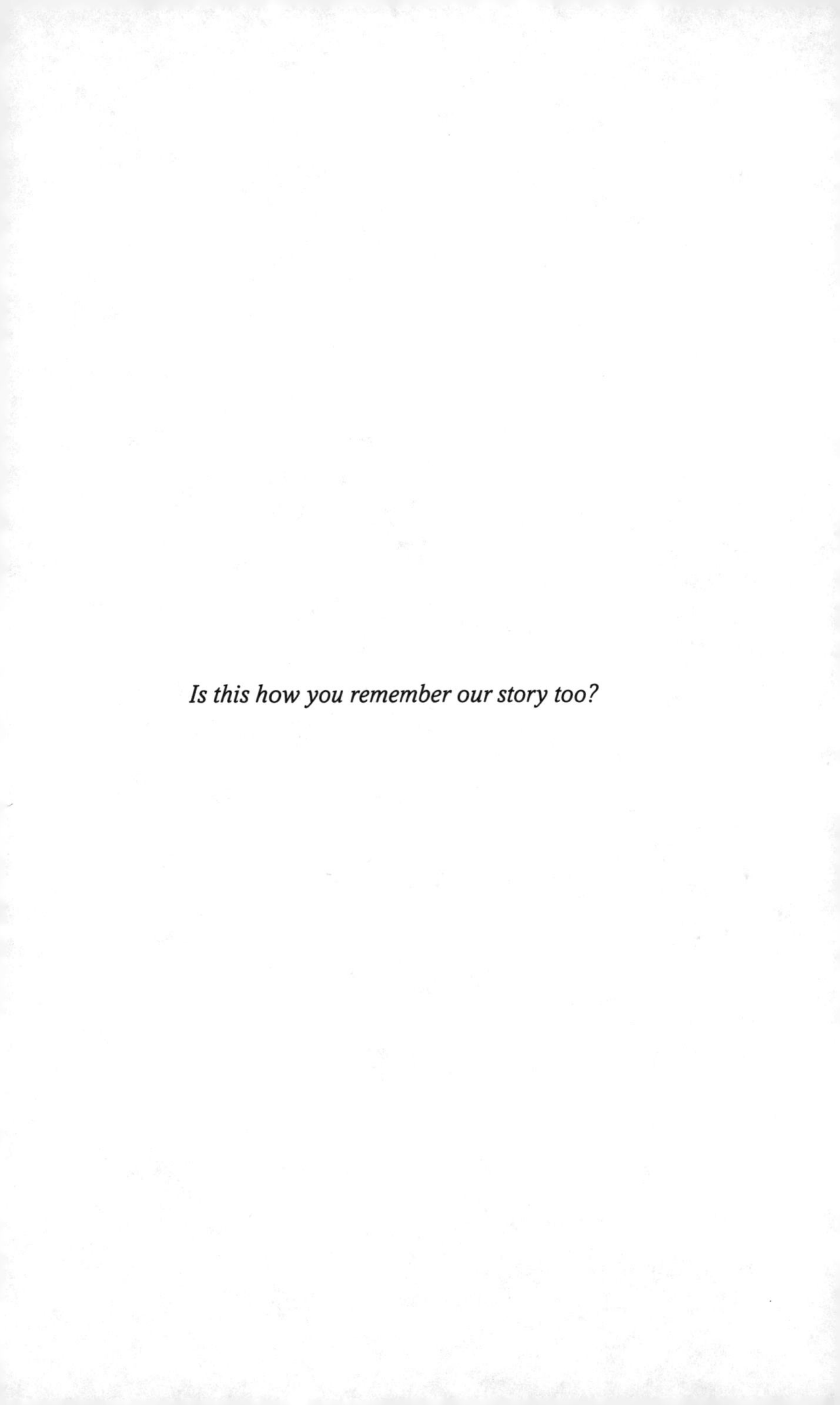
Is this how you remember our story too?

PART I: FOLLOWING YOU

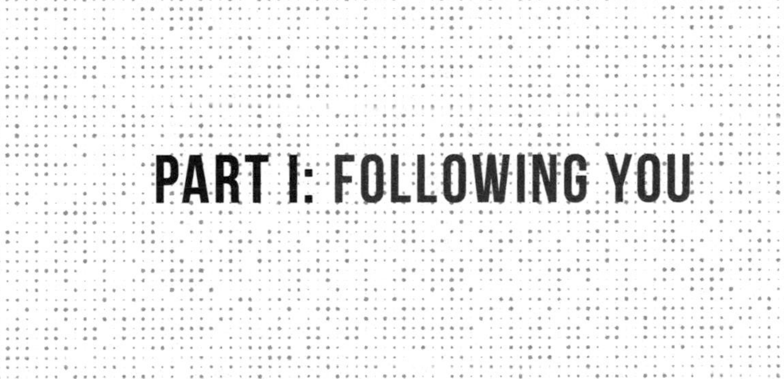

No swiping
No height lies
No tiger pics
No bio quips

Our encounter was
the stuff of urban myths:
an In Real Life sitch.

We met under the desert sky,
strangers among friends
your gaze rested on me
too long for it to be a friendly hi
the sky turned crimson
reading your lingering thoughts
the sun slipped away, so sly
knowing the night is when
lovers unite
stars giggled down
whispering about our fates
finally aligned
I sat, staring up
and you, you only stared
at me that night.

No wait-three-days rule afoot

Desert Bae 😍

Today 11:44 AM

Incoming call/Mobile

27 mins 56 sec

You call, not text
and I think finally
I've found myself
a modern romantic,
someone I could even
make mine.

.

.

.

Or, are you just a friend?

Most people are imitations
of their idols
of favorite characters—
forever editing their lives
to fit an ideal.

Not you:
you are your own being
unaltered, untainted.

You notice things
about me
I did not think
were worth noting.

We hang like friends
and kiss like lovers
I want to know:
what are we?

On a trip away,
your phone battery died.
You added me on Facebook
to make sure I knew why
you hadn't replied.
I wonder maybe,
we have something here,
you and I.

You say my name
and I finally know
what it means
to come undone.

I am no good at jokes:
despite off-delivery, and
references too vague,
you laugh every time
looking into my eyes
making me feel seen
for the first time in my life.

You are
my favorite
notification.

You have turned me into a cliché:
I check if you're online
a dozen times a day
lol at your Snaps
{you'd be such an entertaining date}
and wonder if you tweet about me
or is there some other pizza-loving bae?

Fear and courage, love and lust
feel the same.
Tingling, heart clenching
how to tell, which is what?

I hope
you never
think of
someone else
while you
kiss me.

Lay down your armor
I've cast mine aside
out of these confines
I feel larger, stronger
won't you join me
in this vulnerability?
Let us be true to ourselves
and get to know
each other tonight.

< The Squad
8:10 PM
How's the new bae?
8:08 PM
What bae?
8:09 PM
You both need to get over your commitment issues already!
8:10 PM
Enter Message
SEND

The closer
you try to get
the harder
I'll push you away.

< **Notes** Edit

Dear You,

I fear you because you are so much like me.

I spent years enjoying the chase, growing bored with anything real.

It seemed easier to run away, go on adventures, kiss strangers under the desert sky: pretend that is what it means to live my best life.

I know now, it is not.

I don't think you know yet.

~~Love~~ ~~Yours~~ Always,
Me

I don't want you to go,
you say.

I feel my doubts
melt away.

You want to make me breakfast?
you ask.

My sincerity puzzles you
and it unquiets my heart to know
you have never been loved before.

We love inexpertly
in whispers and gushes
fragments and bursts
never sure
how much to give
never sure
how to take.

You created us
a Netflix profile
naming it our own
version of Brangelina.

You have a quality about you
a gravity,
your eyes dare me to look away
knowing I won't, I can't
because when you look at me
nothing else exists.

Thought fragments
flash images
and a sudden rush
thundering
in my chest
as the air turns heavy
like impending rain.

The feeling of you
l i n g e r s
leaving me electrified
for days.

<Desert Bae
6:50 AM
GN
11:52 PM
Good night, sweet dreams
11:54 PM
Good morning, how'd you sleep?
6:37 AM
Enter Message
SEND

I felt your absence
before I met you
as one misses stars
in a dark night sky—
knowing they are there,
wishing they'd appear.

Saturday night dates
are easy to find
but I want only you
on Sunday mornings.

Weave your fingers with mine
let me rest my head on your chest
stroke my hair and tell me
all your dreams and fears;
let me see your darkness
and I'll show you mine.

We haven't known each other for long
it is probably too early to say
I love you
{but what is love, if not this?}
I tell you I want to know you more,
when I really mean
I no longer want a life
without you in it.

But that would probably scare you.

Instead I ask
where you grew up, ask
about your siblings,
we talk about how much
you miss your mother.

I want to tell you I love you
but maybe it's not the time.
I hope when you look in my eyes,
the way only you know how to,
you see my soul pouring out.

In all my things said, unsaid,
what I really mean to say is
don't ever go.

It's rather risqué, isn't it;
how deeply embedded
you are in my thoughts.

The days have grown
too long
as I wait to see you
and the nights, well
I have never met shorter nights.
The moon must be on strike
or maybe
no amount of time is enough
when I am with you.

Love is relativity and time travel
distortion and dilation
it is when the 1440 minutes in a day
are not all the same length
most are useless
but the few spent with you
are tiny infinities.

In a world
that no longer pauses
to listen to the whispers of a soul
you found songs
I didn't know I held within me.

< The Squad
10:10 AM
You are so in love.
9:54 AM
Maybe I just like the good morning texts…
10:10 AM
Enter Message
SEND

In a starless night, your smile is the moon
as I look within your eyes of purple hue
I see universes of us, in dimensions anew
it seems against the laws of nature
to have a mortal as impeccable as you
we search and search,
to explain body and soul
yet I found you, an irrational whole.
Are you real or a fevered dream;
will you disappear, as I catch my bravery?

Is reality better
or the digital us?

Are you better
or the idea of you?

The thing about love is,
it cannot be ignored.
I can pretend it is
anger, resentment,
jealousy, fear.
I can call it
by different names
but it is here,
as undeniable as the soft pulsing
of blood through my veins.

I feel like someone else
when I am with you
a better someone
a softer me.

As I sit beside you,
coffee warming my hands
your words heating my heart,
my walls disintegrate.

I think I may be
falling in love
with you.

My laughter
tastes different with you;
it pours out like a high waterfall
crashing strong,
words land heavy
between gasps;
it is not an elegant laugh
but I don't care.
You like me messy
so I allow myself to spill over;
these unfiltered moments
are how I measure our love.

Growing up,
love felt like a superstition
a fantasy I should not
indulge in.
Then you came along
providing me faith in something
I had given up on.

If they ask me, *What is love?*,
all I can say is, *you*.
For when we met,
it finally made sense
what others meant
when they spoke of love.

My love is
not a blooming flower
for that shall die too soon
nor is it an ocean fickle
with its affair with the moon
it is not a deeply rooted tree
for they can lie decaying too.

This love of mine is like matter
abundant, ever-present
the kind that cannot be
created nor destroyed
and as this love shifts
its energy to you
treat it gently for
it is pure,
it is true.

I strive every day
to see you as you are,
not as you should be.

In the hours of deepened dusk,
you reek of loneliness
and the burdens of this flesh
as twilight lengthens endlessly
it feels tomorrow may never arrive
there is an urgency in your melancholy
for if death were to visit, it would surely be tonight
alone in these late-night hours when time stands still
your cries of love come tumbling out,
you feel alive at last, flesh on flesh triumphs all.
But what love is that which is born in despair?
Instead, love me in the morning light,
with a fresh promise and hope ahead
when all seems possible, senses erect
in the glory of a new day, love me right.

You are
heartbreaking
and breathtaking
in the sorrows you fight.

I see your faults;
but for the first time
they are not an excuse
to run away.

As you trace figures on my back
I close my eyes and
forget the stresses that gnaw at me
our silence is lavish
glimmering with understanding
you know every etch on my soul.

For the first time, maybe ever,
the storm in my chest softens to a hum
words racing through my brain
turn into wisps of air
as our heartbeats slowly sync,
you settle my turmoil.

You are my
I-wake-up-and-think-of-you
love.

In spaces between breaths
ends of unfinished sentences
stopped at red lights
cruising through greens
loading new Netflix episodes
stirring honey in tea
gazing into eyes
reminiscent of your blues
you steal moments away from me;
I am yours in ways
you do not know
and I give you everything,
willingly.

You will always be safe with me,
you say.

Every night we untie
the knots of situations
put salve on cuts from the day—
no nick too small,
no wound too hideous.

Every morning we prepare
for our circumstances—
with you, I do so with hope.

Some days,
I just cannot face the world alone.

Love me like the ocean loves the shore
sometimes hard, sometimes gentle
retreating a bit to let her breathe
but never too far, never for long.

It was not until I met you
that I understood
I had never been in love before.

My love might be
hard to hear
but I promise
it is here.

How exquisite it is
to have someone want to chase
every thought
meander around each memory lane
and make a home in my brain.

I want to be your favorite book
the one you read over and over again
take me off the shelf, wear me out
{don't worry, I have a strong spine}
understand my heartbreaks
stain me with your tears
dog-ear your favorite bits
take notes, memorize details
read between my lines
find new meaning every time
make me your favorite book,
because you are mine.

Do you feel it too?
We have such a connection,
you say.

Yes, it scares me
how similar we are,
I reply.

< **Notes** Edit

Dear You,

It is equally frightening:
to know this may be forever
to know you may leave at any moment.

Still not ready to say love out loud,
Me

We were sipping tea, watching rain fall
when you whispered above the storm,
Aristotle believed the sound of thunder
was the clash of two clouds.
That may have been when
I fell in love with you.
Or maybe it was our sunrise walks
turning this night owl chipper at dawn.

People say, *Don't let someone change you*,
but how can we not change
with every encounter
every relationship
every love?

We take a bit of someone
give a bit of us away.
I have changed since your love
and I like
who I have become.

In the clouds
and tea leaves,
the ink blots
and tarot cards
all I ever see is
you and me.

Love me
like the world loves
Beyoncé.

In a world so determined
to sort us in boxes—
are you happy or sad
a morning person or night
woke warrior or shy
brown or white?

In a world that forgets
how ridiculous it is for a being
to be just one thing
when we are stardust and earth,
ashes and flowers
all mangled together.

In a world that demands
I piece myself apart
to claim one identity or another,
I only find myself whole, here
with you, I can be everything,
I can be me.

I want a house filled with
paintings, books, sunflower dust,
and whispers from you.

Perhaps we should discuss love
but that is a topic for volumes
and I probably don't have
enough phone battery.

< **Notes** Edit

Dear You,

Do you feel the same about me?
I have so much to say,
but do you want to listen?
Do you hold back your affection
because you do not know
how much I care?

I wonder what it would be like
if we, for once, told each other
what we truly feel.
I have never been good at reading
"the signs."

Maybe I am ready to tell you
I love you.
Maybe it doesn't matter
if you don't say it back.

Nervously,
Me

With you, the commitments of love
no longer seem burdensome.

< The Squad
3:31 PM
Are you two official yet?
2:34 PM
We don't talk about those things.
3:01 PM
So...FWB?
3:30 PM
Enter Message
SEND

I do not understand you
but that does not worry me;
I barely understand myself.

< **Notes** Edit

Dear You,

Are you here to stay? I cannot tell.
There are days when I am sure,
others when you are
nowhere to be found.
Is it me?

I am often accused of being
closed off, unavailable
you see, I don't like public declarations
{or even private ones}
but it's not the same with you.

For the first time I can say
post our selfies
update the relationship status
tag me

I'll even tell you my password.

Ready for Love,
Me

If you want to be with me
you will make it happen;
there is no bad timing
just excuses.

I didn't know you wear glasses,
you say.

Only for reading, I reply,
wondering
who have you been looking at
all this time.

< New Message
Desert Bae
Are you seeing other people?
SEND
I
Or
I'm
q w e r t y u i o p
a s d f g h j k l
z x c v b n m
123
?
space
return

Your attention is manic
I wither away, like a peony
under darkened skies
forgetting the touch of your light
for long stretches at a time,
yet I await your return.

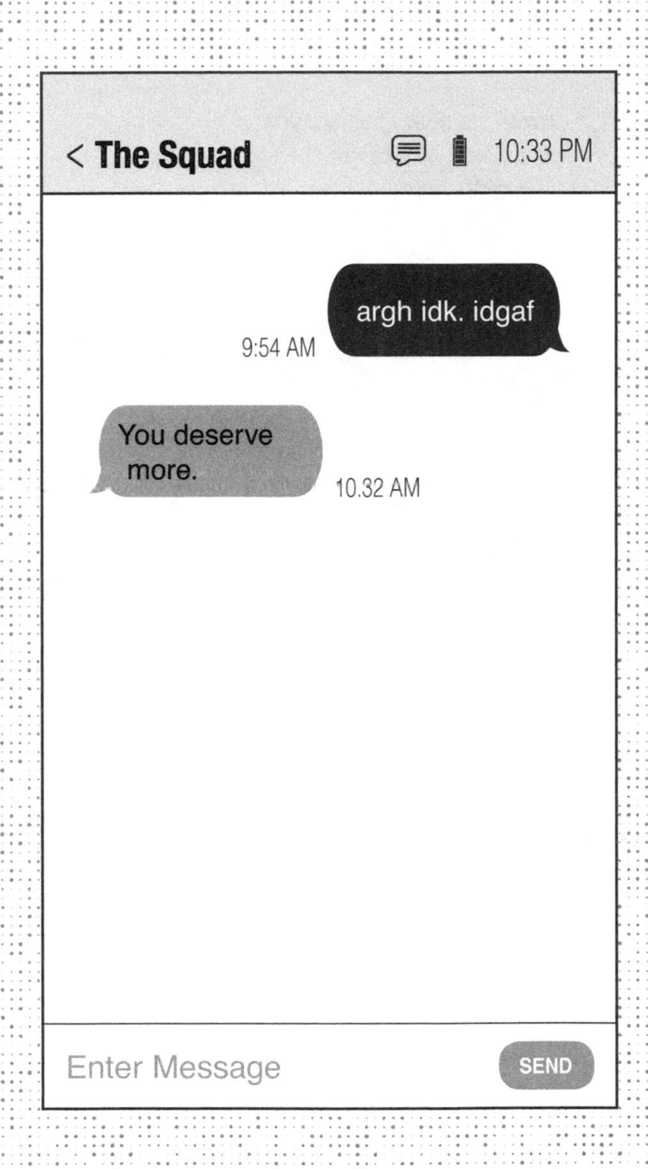
< The Squad
10:33 PM
argh idk. idgaf
9:54 AM
You deserve more.
10.32 AM
Enter Message
SEND

How can someone like you
like someone like me?
you ask.

How are you fine
handing me all your sorrows
unwilling to take any of mine?

You lost signal
in the middle of the sentence.
I waited by the phone
yet you never called back,
but I saw updates
on your Instagram.

I have been swallowing
these words for far too long
I just need to say aloud

I love you.

I have been hurt before,
you reply.
Can we take it slow?
I care for you.

I understand,
I lie.

PART II: UNFOLLOWING YOU

Who needs labels?
you ask.
Let's just get to know each other.

Sure,
I lie
when I should say
goodbye.

And like last-minute work
skipped workouts
decent bedtime,
leaving you becomes
another thing I put off.

In the end,
it is the things I do willingly
that weigh on me most.

Love leaves in missed good mornings
and forgotten coffee orders;
it is always the small things
that matter most.

My desire for you grew
yours for me faltered
and that should have
been the end.

I understand the comfort
in empty promises.
Like drinking Shasta,
pretending it's Coca-Cola.

I question
your intentions
never
your goodness.

I pour happiness
to water your soul
but nothing works
I must let you go
I cannot bear it anymore,
how you love
your sadness more.

< The Squad
9:45 PM
Are you still seeing each other?
9:42 PM
Sometimes...we both really like each other.
9:44 PM
Enter Message
SEND

It is a constant battle:
walking towards
walking away
from you.

I miss you, you say.

I convince myself,
you just need more time.

I cannot love you
I will not love you
I shall not love you
these silent reveries
stay with me all day
because I can tell
this love will destroy me
and though
it is nothing I cannot survive
I am too tired
to keep this uncertainty alive
so just leave
or stay
whichever you choose,
do it all the way.

I am drowning
in the shallow waters
of your affection.

There should have been more.

There is a light felt in the embrace of love
a cozy pastel or shimmery gold
but you are neon red
the pause-and-go of a fast-food joint
your words synthetic sweet
infused with corn syrup lies;
there is nothing natural about you
your freshly thawed words
dished out in mass supply.

I'm lovin' you, you say
to every new bae, I learn too late.
If I had paid more attention
I would've tasted your artificial ways.
Even as greener pastures beckon
I want to stay for just one more taste;
a glutton for your temporary love,
this naive sin nourishes me today.

You reach for me in your sadness and
I forget I cannot lift you out of it
I forget you want to pull me down
just for the company.

Intimacy makes friendships stronger,
you say.

The man karaokeing on stage gets louder
Good times never seem so good, he drones on
I look around, wondering if someone would
tell the man he's singing too loud
the man must know, he's in the wrong.

We should go to my place,
you say.

I feel the salt at the back of my throat
threatening to pour out,
then pity pricks my eyes as I realize
you are missing the point of it all, this life
the bliss in calling one person your own.

I imagined
a hundred things
I wanted to do with you.

You imagined
a hundred things
you wanted to do to me.

Sorry I placed so much
value on your words.
You see,
I thought you meant them.

Time with you now feels
like a trip to Taco Bell;
great in the moment
regretful the next day.

I missed you, you'd say
even though we'd texted
all day.
Back when you remembered
the things I told you
and asked questions,
quickly learning
about me.

When you have me
you cannot be bothered
to look my way.
Do you remember
when we fell in love?
I do.
The memories are
the only thing
that keep me tethered
as we drift apart.

But I am learning,
slowly learning,
those are not enough.
I untie their knots around me,
slowly learning
the art of moving on.

Madness is no notifications
and a Read.

Humans should come with
macronutrients & warning labels

Yours:
35% goodness
65% evil
9 grams of kindness
32 grams of bullshit

Beware: dangerous to consume,
lethal to love.

Well dear, I suppose
you don’t really know me
for all you do
is talk about you.

Slowly,
you seem to be
like everyone else in the city.
Looking over my shoulder
to see who else is in the room.
Wanting to be
someplace more exciting,
with someone more exciting.
I begin to envy
the bald eagles,
the alligators
whose monogamy
comes without thought.

I am a master at self-deception;
I believe in your words of love
even as I stare at your eyes of lust.

I am not ready for a commitment,
you say.
I am sorry.

The silence is dense
with condensation from your words
clinging to our faces,
a rotten-sweet stench envelops us.
You look away from me and
I wonder if you can feel
the quake in my chest,
if you can hear
the roar of my heart.

You sit silently,
I feel each limb fall apart.
Yet I stand up, willing my organs
to continue functioning, my bones
to remain twined and carry me out.
I have no words left
perhaps my swollen tongue
may never utter another word again.

I gather up my limbs
and organs and bones
and hope and dignity and love
and drag them out the door.

< The Squad
8:16 PM
Did you finally say I love you?
8:15 PM
We unfriended each other.
8:16 PM
Enter Message
SEND

I extended my world to you
shyly, heaving under its weight.
How casually you turned it down,
like extra butter on popcorn.

.

.

.

{only monsters do that;
now you know what I think of you}

I envy people who can talk of love
calmly, casually
like discussing a favorite app or brand,
as if it is something everyone has.

You said sorry without
understanding why,
that is when I should've known
I needed to let you go.

Sweetly, profusely
you always apologized.
His work is difficult, I'd say,
he is so sorry.
They shook their heads
and muttered, *Again?*

And then there were
too many missed dates
and forgotten promises.

I had to admit,
your apologies were a blanket
to smother my questions.

I had to admit
you never cared to know
what was wrong.

I had to admit
you never intended to stay.

Some nights I stay up wondering
what you are escaping or looking for
in the different beds you spend your time.
Are you trying to forget
the pain of a love unreturned
or are you searching for an old lover
in new faces every night?

Tell me, why wasn't I enough?

< Don't Bother
2:02 AM
You up?
2:01 AM
Nope.
2:02 AM
Enter Message
SEND

I am not your vacation home,
your place away from reality.
I'm flesh, blood, feelings, emotions,
not a piece of realty.

Don't ever forget that.

I see updates of you
in rooms I no longer recognize,
Insta stories with strangers
{new baes, I wonder?}
Even offline
you remain on my mind.

IN A RELATIONSHIP

Comment

Maybe what hurts most
is how easy I was to get over.
How you have another
before the goodbye has begun.

Look what you made me do:

TINDER REACTIVATED

Others are gentle and listen
caring I have never known,
yet my heart races
only at thoughts of you.

I am trying to learn
how to mourn
the loss of something
that never really was.

I am insufferable to be around;
I get myself drunk on thoughts of you
and vomit out words of us
from an imagination overused.

I worry about unfilled cravings
uncorrected mistakes,
I worry about me, without you.

I have photos of you, of us
tucked away beneath jumbled socks.
There is one of you writing at that diner
we sat at for hours.
I cannot see your eyes but your smile,
I look at it when I'm blue.

Did you keep mine too?
Send me some, I want to see
what you captured of me.
That is who I am, that me with you.
I would rather be remembered
through your eyes
than mine.

Stray glances and last-minute hangs,
the signs were there all along
I chose to ignore gut instinct
and carried on with fledgling hope—
I saw so much of me in you.

I waited for you to recognize
what we had was special
maybe, different,
but you had blindfolds on as well.

It must have been in my most
egotistical of moods
when I believed you loved me too.

< **Notes** Edit

Dear You,

Do you ever text me?
I wouldn't know,
I blocked you days ago.

Do you know,
you are still the first person
I want to share good news with?

Without you, life feels emptier.

Just,
Me

When they ask you about love,
does my name ever come up?

I swallow words,
sticky sour
like mornings of beer
and tobacco aftertastes.

Sticky sour words
that turn into land mines
when kept too long
words exploding, uncaring
of celebrations or joy,
of time or resolve.

Sticky sour words
that I cannot scrape off.
Do not ask questions
for which answers
you aren't prepared to hear
—I remind myself.
But in the not knowing
I find my madness.

Maybe the hardest part
is letting myself feel the pain,
acknowledging
you had meant something
we had meant something.

At least to me.

Despite it all, I admire your work;
how beautifully you destroyed
first my walls, then me.

It is the silences I miss the most:
driving down winding lanes
destination unknown,
inhaling the crispness of trees
sitting on bar stools
with music too loud for conversation,
lying slumped against my staircase
unable to speak all the words
corroding my insides.
You were always there
and my silences had a home.

In moments of stillness
it is still your page I refresh.

< **Notes** Edit

Dear You,

You often accused me of overthinking,
of questioning too much,
caring too much.

I should have realized then,
this would never work.
Because the fact is, maybe
you do not think enough.

If you do not assess what is said to you,
what you are conveying to another,
why bother a deep connection,
the time indulgence?

It is not up to me to tell you to strive
for deeper relationships.
But it does not mean I will tolerate
your surface-level show.

Processing,
Me

Your love had a
limited vocabulary.

Your wants.
Your needs.

There were no
words in your dictionary
defining how to love me.

You never claimed to love me,
I thank you for that.

In the end, I blame myself
for believing something
never said.

Now I am left with doubt
on what was truly felt.

Your words were like poetry
{or maybe your lips}
you knew how to swing
the pendulum of emotion
sometimes like Neruda
sometimes like Poe
at times, we were a fairy tale
at times, a horror show.

I hoarded your love
from the very beginning
as if I knew
it'd be in limited supply.

Hundreds of photos of you
of us
numbering far more
than the days we spent together
a box full of memorabilia.
I have made something
out of the nothings you gave me.

I am good at giving meaning
to words that held no feeling
to things that were meant to be
discarded from the beginning
I am too good at trying on love
that was never my fit.

I break my own heart a few times
before understanding it is over.
I wake up excited, forgetting
the empty side, the parted lover.

Let me be clear, I did not need you;
but oh how much I wanted you.

I now see how unoriginal our love was:
you—full of pickup lines
me—a bundle of poetry.

I took responsibility
for your emotions,
that was my mistake.

You let me,
and that was yours.

< Notes Edit

Dear You,

Someone asked about you.
I began to tell them
when I last spoke to you,
you still believed in me the most.

I had told you I was lost
in the realities of responsibilities
you told me that I was a dream
and dreams are not bound
to realities or nationalities,
dreams create their own path as they go
and dreams can be more real
than anything in this material world.

You told me to live in my dreams
till they become reality.

And even as the words
were coming out of me,
I realized I was too dreamlike
for you to create a reality with me.

You said all the right things
but never at the right time.
You did not want to dream with me,
I understand that now.
I still love you very much,
I understand this too.

Hiding,
Me

It feels unfair,
the act of will
required to leave you
when falling in love
was never a choice.

The brain is inaccurately
likened to an operating system.
See if this was an OS
I could block certain terms
like your name,
from popping in memory
a defaulted screensaver
when my brain is on pause.

It should be a universal law:
when two people are together
their love for each other must equal out.
Maybe like gravity or motion
perhaps finite math—anything tangible.
Because I am tired of loving someone
more than they love me.

The more I learn of you
the less I love you.
In the end, they were right
all I needed was time.

Even with eyes burning
I remind myself
this sting won't last.
As the smoke clears,
thoughts of you
will be long gone.

There is no shore, no safe house
unless I seek them.
If I only focus on the water
I will continue to drown.

I didn't see what you really were
till you had taken all my light,
forever collapsing within yourself
still hungry for more.

I have no words of love left for you,
keep that heart you ripped out of me
you must need it more;
I am growing another.

It took me years to unlearn
love is a weakness
I will not allow you
to be that lesson again.

The last few times I saw you,
I hadn't been able to look into your eyes.
They pulled me in,
pulled out the emotion in me
And I would drown in the feeling,
knowing you didn't love me.
knowing I still loved you.

Now, I look into your eyes;
were they always this dark?
I swear I remember
speckles of gold and green
a glimmer, a sheen
or maybe it was a dream.

I look at them now,
uninterrupted by emotions
and my heart settles
into quiet indifference.

This, I realize, is moving on.

There was a time
I couldn't tell me
from you.

Now, I am glad
I am with me
while you are with you.

How does it feel
to no longer be
my favorite notification?

< The Squad
8:17 PM
Try Bumble
8:15 PM
Let new love into your life.
You deserve it. ❤
8:16 PM
Enter Message
SEND

< **Notes** Edit

Dear Me,

Do not try so hard not to feel something
that you no longer feel anything.
The pain may seem unbearable,
a loneliness that leaves the soul trembling
a chill that feels like it is here to stay,
but do not let the ice set in.

Feel it all.

You must bear the pain so you know
what happiness is, when it comes.
Because it will come.
I promise, it will.

Love,
Me

I burrow deeper within
digging out big hurts and small
hands raw, fingers bleeding
ears ringing from broken love.

I burrow deeper within
hauling out carcasses
devouring demons whole
mouth full of tales untold.

I burrow deeper within
to unseen tunnels for solemn healing
creating a path to new hope
making myself a home.

< **Notes** Edit

Dear You,

There is something I wish you to know:

It does not matter if
you remember me fondly,
or not at all.

It does not matter if
you wish me well,
or forget me altogether.

But if you feel the urge
to look me up
to text me
to DM me,
don't bother.

Letting go,
Me

Alone, I feel clean
without you, I am back to me.

< The Squad
11:12 PM
There will be someone who understands you even better. Who'll love you like we do!
11:12 PM
Enter Message
SEND

< **Notes** Edit

Dear Me,

You deserve someone
who makes an effort
who appreciates your uniqueness
who reminds you of your beautiful spirit
who respects and admires you
who challenges and inspires you.

Your bones carry stories
of strength untold
my darling, all of you
deserves to be known.

Find someone who stays because
they couldn't imagine a life without you.

Don't settle for less.

Love,
Me

There is a rumble
of change
within me

I sit in it
drown in it
then, transform.

The electricity of new synapses
courses through my brain
bending shooting stars my way.
I wish on each of them,
step over their dust trails
jump into wishing wells
drown out hate
swim in gratitude
luck vibrating
in every atom.
I cannot wait
to emerge anew.

Watching "our shows" without you,
that is moving on.

I no longer wonder
what it would be like
to build a life with you.

I can unfollow you now.

ABOUT THE AUTHOR

Komal Kapoor is a Los Angeles-based writer, business consultant, and motivational coach. Originally from Punjab, India, she moved to the United States when she was 10 years old. Her passions include painting, travelling, studying behavioral science, helping people be more themselves, and spreading smiles. She explores the messy business of feelings via Instagram—you can follow her journey @komalesque.

ACKNOWLEDGMENTS

My darling family: thank you for allowing me to soar far and close.

Kirsty, Patty, and Susan: thank you for believing in my vision.

Aparna, Drew, Kevin, Lindsay, Nisha, Nyasha, and all other dear friends: thank you for being my confidantes and keeping me sane throughout the years.

My lovely Instagram readers: I have you to thank the most. I started sharing my writing online at a difficult time in my life, and your love was beyond anything I could have ever imagined. Your comments, messages, encouragement, and support made this book happen, and I am forever grateful. Much love, always.

UNFOLLOWING YOU

Andrews McMeel Publishing
a division of Andrews McMeel Universal
1130 Walnut Street, Kansas City, Missouri 64106

www.andrewsmcmeel.com

19 20 21 22 23 BVG 10 9 8 7 6 5 4 3 2 1

ISBN: 978-1-4494-9960-0

Library of Congress Control Number: 2018962796

Editor: Patty Rice
Designer/Art Director: Diane Marsh
Production Editor: Margaret Daniels
Production Manager: Cliff Koehler